TRUTH or BUST

FEMALE PHARAOHS WORE FALSE BEARDS!

The fact or fiction behind EGYPTIANS

Kay Barnham

WAYLAND

First published in 2014 by Wayland

Copyright © Wayland 2014

Wayland
338 Euston Road
London NW1 3BH

Wayland Australia
Level 17/207 Kent Street
Sydney, NSW 2000

Editor: Debbie Foy
Design: Rocket Design (East Anglia) Ltd
Illustration: Alex Paterson

A catalogue record for this book is available from the British Library.
ISBN: 978 0 7502 8133 1
eBook ISBN: 978 0 7502 8726 5
Dewey ref: 932-dc23

Printed in China
10 9 8 7 6 5 4 3 2 1

Wayland is a division of Hachette Children's Books,
an Hachette UK company
www.hachette.co.uk

All illustrations by Shutterstock, except 4, 9, 15, 18, 24, 28, 32, 39, 50-51, 56-57, 62, 69, 70, 75, 76, 83.

DIG DEEP AND FIND OUT THE **TRUTH** ABOUT THE ANCIENT EGYPTIANS

read on!

Read this bit first...!

When you think about Ancient Egypt, what pops into your head? Gruesome mummies? Spooky tombs? Perhaps you're completely wowed by pyramids! But what do you really know about this ancient civilisation?

Just hanging out with Tut...

Let's start with some totally true facts...

 Ancient Egypt was founded over 5,000 years ago, on the banks of the River Nile.

 The country was ruled by pharaohs, who were like kings or queens, but were actually thought of as living gods.

 Pyramids weren't just incredible stone structures, they were actually burial tombs for pharaohs.

 'Pharaoh' is a VERY tricky word to spell.

But, of course, there's more to Ancient Egypt than this. It's a civilisation that's packed with more stories, myths and legends than there are stones in a pyramid. Probably. (And there are a lot of stones in a pyramid. The Great Pyramid of Giza has 2,300,000 of them.)

In fact, so many myths and legends surround Ancient Egypt that it can be hard to work out what's true and what isn't. Did Ancient Egyptians really sell themselves as slaves? Did Cleopatra bathe in milk? And what exactly is the curse of Tutankhamun's tomb?

Time machine out of fuel? Don't worry! This book will whizz you back to the Egypt of long ago and help you to separate the fact from the fiction about one of the greatest civilisations EVER.

(But watch out for flesh-burrowing worms, OK...?)

read on!

So you might hear myths like...

The Ancient Egyptians invented sweets

Really? Surely the Ancient Egyptians were far too busy building pyramids to spend time messing about with chocolate buttons and fruity chews?

⭐ And the truth is...

Not at all. The first known sweets were made in Ancient Egypt around 1600 BCE. But they weren't like the sweets you might eat. Recipes engraved onto stone tablets show that Ancient Egyptian sweets were made from dates, nuts and spices. And — because sugar wasn't invented until much, much later — they were sweetened with honey. They're still sold in the Middle East today. (But not the same ones, obviously. They went off centuries ago...)

Verdict: ⸻ TRUTH ⸻

Egypt was built by Egyptologists

D'oh. Of course it was. Wasn't it?

★ And the truth is...

No, it wasn't.

Egyptology is the study of Ancient Egypt and Egyptologists are people who study Ancient Egypt. They didn't build it. That was the Ancient Egyptians.

But it's because of Egyptology that we know such a lot about Ancient Egypt, its history, its language, its people and much, much more besides.

Verdict: **BUSTED**

PSSST! Most words with an -ology on the end mean the study of something. So 'Egyptology' is the study of Ancient Egypt, 'criminology' is the study of crime and 'palaeontology' is the study of dinosaurs. 'Apology' isn't the study of anything though. Sorry.

> ## Anyone who entered Tutankhamun's tomb was cursed FOR EVER!

Tutankhamun, or King Tut, if you knew him well, was a pharaoh who ruled Egypt from about 1332 to 1323 BCE. (It was a very long time ago and no one is totally sure about the dates.)

When he died aged just 19, Tutankhamun was mummified, like all important Egyptians. (This was a way of preserving the body. See page 48 to find out the gruesome details of how it was done.) Then his body was placed in a tomb in the Valley of the Kings, a popular pharaoh burial site near modern-day Luxor. And there Tutankhamun lay…

… and lay and lay and lay…

… until 1922 CE, over 3,000 years later. That's when the tomb was discovered by English archaeologist and Egyptologist Howard Carter.

There was HUGE excitement, until the members of Howard Carter's expedition began to die in Very Mysterious Circumstances…

WHY? Was the tomb cursed?!

⭐ And the truth is...

It's certainly true that Lord Carnarvon, who had paid for the expedition, died from a mosquito bite in 1932. His death was immediately blamed on the mummy's curse. And from then on, whenever ANYONE connected with the expedition died, the curse was held responsible. When the two pilots who brought Tutankhamun's artefacts to London died from heart attacks, it was because of the mummy. And when the curator of the museum in Cairo where the pharaoh's treasures were stored was hit by a car and killed... that was Tutankhamun's fault too.

Even when a member of the expedition died at the age of 101, which was hardly unexpected, a newspaper said that the mummy's curse was to blame.

And what about Howard Carter himself? He died in 1939, from natural causes.

Almost certainly, definitely and absolutely

Verdict: **BUSTED** (Probably)

10

A pharaoh once used his slaves as human flypaper

No way.

Surely even the pottiest pharaoh wouldn't think of doing that?

★ And the truth is...

Oh yes they did.

Pharaoh Pepi II became ruler of Egypt when he was just six years old, and perhaps so much power at such a young age made him go a bit silly. He was particularly bothered by flies and came up with a totally bonkers solution.

He made sure that there were always a few slaves nearby — naked and smothered in honey — to attract flies and stop them from bothering him.

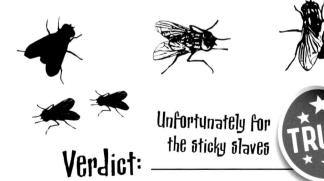

Verdict: Unfortunately for the sticky slaves **TRUTH**

11

Ancient Egyptians sold themselves as slaves

It wasn't much fun being a slave in Ancient Egypt. If you were lucky, you might be a servant, a dancer or even an acrobat for a wealthy Egyptian. But there was also a risk you'd be sent to work on a farm or down a mine. And, if you were REALLY unlucky, you'd get to be human flypaper. (Seriously. See page 11 to find out more.)

So surely slavery wasn't a life that anyone would choose voluntarily...?

★ And the truth is...

Some people were so short of cash that they sold members of their own families into slavery.* Some people were kidnapped from other countries and then sold. Others were prisoners of war, who were then forced into slavery. And, yes, some people sold THEMSELVES, to pay off debts or to escape from poverty.

Yikes.

Verdict:  ——— TRUTH ———

*Ahem. This is now STRICTLY ILLEGAL and DEFINITELY NOT a way of getting rid of a brother or sister. Not even if they are REALLY annoying.

HOW THE ANCIENT EGYPTIANS CURED

POOR EYESIGHT!

 You will need: A pig's eye, a teaspoon of honey, a teaspoon of red ochre (a natural colouring that contains a heap of iron oxide), a pestle and mortar, a bucket.

Method: Grind up the pig's eye. (If this bit makes you feel thoroughly QUEASY, then keep the bucket handy.)

Loosen the mixture with honey.

Finally, add red ochre. (It probably won't make the medicine any more effective, but at least it'll be a lovely colour.)

How to treat the patient: Dollop the mixture into your patient's ear. It doesn't matter that you're actually supposed to be treating their eyesight. This medicine is guaranteed to be so useless that it'll have zero effect wherever you stick it.

PHARAOH PHACT PHILE

FULL NAME: Ramesses II, also known as Ramesses the Great

NATIONALITY: Egyptian

LIVED: 1303–1213 BCE

REIGNED: 1279–1213 BCE

WIVES: Ramesses did way better than Henry VIII. He had no less than EIGHT royal wives during his reign, but he had two favourites. Nefertari gave birth to Ramesses' son and heir (as well as plenty of other princes and princesses) and he must have been pretty keen on her because Nefertari's tomb in the Valley of the Queens was – and still is – beauuuuutiful. Isinofre gave Ramesses his second son (and yet more children) and replaced Nefertari as Top Queen after she died.

CHILDREN: LOTS. (See page 16 to find out more.)

WHO WAS RAMESSES?

He was Egypt's most famous pharaoh. Ramesses II reigned for 66 years, built countless cities, temples and monuments all over Egypt, signed the world's first peace treaty and conquered many lands and kingdoms.

MOST FAMOUS FOR?

Being great. He wasn't called *Ramesses the Great* for nothing, you know!

King Ramesses II had 200 children

Ramesses II was one of the longest-ruling pharaohs of Ancient Egypt. And, according to the inscriptions on his monuments, he was pretty good in a battle situation too.

But was Ramesses II really one of the most successful daddies of all time...?

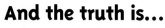 **And the truth is...**

Ramesses II had at least eight wives. So his chances of having a big family were fairly high. But the exact number of children that he actually fathered is unknown.

Luckily, the images and names of many of his offspring are carved on several monuments, which has led experts to guess that he may have had as many as 56 sons and 44 daughters, making a grand total of 100. Some reports put the number much higher, at 200. But experts think that Ramesses actually had about 160 children.

Wow. Imagine having to remember THAT many birthdays!

Verdict:

Go on, YOU can decide this time.

PSSST! Ramesses II reigned for 67 years, which is one of the reasons he earned the nickname Ramesses the Great. When he died aged 90, he was buried in the Valley of the Kings. But because this was a hotspot for tomb raiders, he was later moved to a different burial spot – next to Queen Inhapy – to keep him safe. Later, he was shifted to the Egyptian Museum in Cairo.

The daddy of all mummies is still there today.

EGYPTIAN BABY NAMES

No, no. I insist. It's YOUR turn.

Ramesses II's mummy had its own passport

Ramesses II (or Ramesses the Great to you and I) might have escaped the Valley of the Kings in one piece, but in 1974, he faced a brand new danger. Curators at the Egyptian Museum in Cairo were horrified to see that the mummy was going ROTTEN.

The only answer, of course, was to fly the pharaoh to Paris, for emergency treatment. But surely he wouldn't need a passport to fly to France, would he? After all, he'd been DEAD for over 3,000 years...?

⭐ And the truth is...

Rules were rules. Without a passport, Ramesses II wasn't going ANYWHERE. So he was given his very own Egyptian passport, with his occupation listed as: *King (deceased)*. And at Le Bourget Airport near Paris, he was given a reception fit for a, erm... king.

It turned out that as well as being a king (deceased), Ramesses was a king (diseased) too, because experts discovered that he was being attacked by a nasty green fungus.

The fungus was treated — hurray! — and Ramesses II returned to Egypt, a happy mummy.

Verdict:

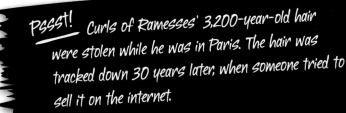

Pssst! Curls of Ramesses' 3,200-year-old hair were stolen while he was in Paris. The hair was tracked down 30 years later, when someone tried to sell it on the internet.

19

Female pharaohs wore false beards

Does a beard really suit me?

In Ancient Egypt, most men shaved (to find out why, see page 74). But a beard was supposed to show that its owner was really god-like, and a pharaoh couldn't miss the opportunity to look even more important than he was already, so he wore a FAKE beard made of goat hair, because that was somehow less trouble than, um, growing the real thing.

But what about female pharaohs?

Surely *they* wouldn't bother with a beard?

Wouldn't it look a bit ODD?

⭐ And the truth is...

At least one female pharaoh DID wear a beard.

Hatshepsut (1508–1458 BCE) was first a queen of Egypt, reigning with her husband, Thutmose II. Then when he died, she decided she would be pharaoh herself. And she was VERY good at it. And by and large her reign was a happy one, in which the Ancient Egyptians made temples and monuments, not war.

Hatshepsut wore a fake beard like male pharaohs simply to show that she was in charge.

Verdict:  TRUTH

PSSST!   A pharaoh couldn't wear any old beard, of course. A goatee was out. So was a big bushy number in the style of Blackbeard the pirate. Instead, the pharaoh wore a long, straight beard that widened at the bottom like a kipper tie.

But a tightly plaited beard was the most god-like chin ornament of all. And dead pharaohs were often shown wearing a narrow rope-like beard with a bend at the bottom, a little like the foot at the bottom of a fancy chair leg.

Aliens built the pyramids

The theory is that ancient astronauts visited Earth thousands of years ago, to give Earthlings a helping hand. It's said that these aliens helpfully boosted human DNA to make people cleverer.

What's more, the ancient alien astronauts are said to have given a hand with some of the really magnificent structures from long ago, like the pyramids. Because the pyramids were clearly FAR too tricky for the Ancient Egyptian humanoids to have built all on their own.

★ And the truth is...

Some people DO believe that this is true. But apart from a mural inside a tomb that could show an alien (but probably shows a vase) and some gaps in historical records (which is obviously when the aliens came visiting), there is no real evidence.

Meanwhile, many, many more people believe that even though the pyramids must have been fiendishly difficult to build without modern construction techniques and cranes and diggers and calculators and hundreds of civil engineers, the Ancient Egyptians were more than capable of having a go.

Verdict: $\dfrac{99.99999999\%}{}$ **BUSTED**

HOW THE ANCIENT EGYPTIANS CURED

BALDNESS!

You will need: *Ox fat, Lion fat, Hippo fat, Goose fat, Snake fat, Cat fat, Crocodile fat, Ibex fat, Serpent fat.*

So, basically, lots of fat. And a big spoon.

And an even bigger bowl.

Method: *Mix all the different types of fat together.*

Ta-daaaaa. That's it. You're done!

How to treat the patient: *Smear the mixture over the bald head. (Ask first.) Be generous! After all, you've probably made enough gloop to treat the head of every pharaoh who ever lived.*

Whether you actually make their hair grow or not is another matter.*

*Let's face it. Probably not.

The Ancient Egyptians played Snakes and Ladders

Well, there were more than enough snakes in Egypt — just ask Cleopatra (see page 27)! So perhaps the Ancient Egyptians DID play the game that's still popular today! Maybe they even invented it!

And the truth is…

★ And the truth is…

Nearly, but not quite.

The Ancient Egyptians actually played a board game called Dogs and Jackals. The game worked by moving small stick figures in the shape of — you guessed it — dogs and jackals into the holes dotted around a board, which was decorated with a palm tree.

But because it didn't catch on like Snakes and Ladders, the only reason we know about Dogs and Jackals is because a fancy board game and ten tiny figures were discovered in an Ancient Egyptian tomb.

Verdict: —— BUSTED ——

Pssst! Snakes and Ladders actually came from Ancient India, where it was called Moksha Patam.

Cleopatra wasn't Egyptian

Er... what? Ancient Egypt's last pharaoh, famous for her beauty, her men — top Romans Julius Caesar and Mark Antony — and her death supposedly by asp bite (see opposite page for more details on this) wasn't actually from Egypt?

★ And the truth is...

Cleopatra might have been from Egypt, but her family was Greek. The Ptolemaic dynasty ruled Egypt for nearly three centuries, until the Romans took over in 30 BCE.

While they were in power, the Ptolemies insisted on speaking Greek — except Cleopatra. She DID learn to speak Egyptian.

Verdict: sort of  TRUTH (ancestrally speaking)

Cleopatra died from an asp bite

Cleopatra famously finished herself off by holding an asp to her skin. When the creature took a bite, she is said to have died from the poisonous venom that flowed into her bloodstream.

★ And the truth is...

Well, that's what William Shakespeare said in *Antony and Cleopatra*.

With thy sharp teeth this knot intrinsicate
Of life at once untie: poor venomous fool
Be angry, and dispatch.

The thing is, Shakespeare's play was based on information supplied by Ancient Greek biographer, Plutarch. But as Plutarch lived 130 years after Cleopatra died, his story isn't entirely reliable.

In 2010, German historian Christoph Schaefer announced that he had read a lot of ancient texts and spoken to a lot of toxicologists — experts in poison — and revealed that Cleopatra had actually died from a mixture of deadly poisons.

And not an asp.

Verdict: Probably  BUSTED

★ And the truth is...

Cleopatra's Needle isn't the sort of thing you'd want to stick into a sock or a frock that needs mending. It's actually not a needle at all, but an obelisk — a tall, tapering column of stone with a pyramid shape on top.

But guess what...? There isn't just one Cleopatra's Needle. There are three more of them. And none has anything to do with Cleopatra, because they are a 1,000 years older than Ancient Egypt's famous pharaoh. They were actually built during the reign of Thutmose III. Made of granite, each is covered with Egyptian hieroglyphs that honour Ramesses II.

Verdict:  _____

Pssst! Look out for Cleopatra's Needles on London's South Bank, in the Place de la Concorde in Paris and in New York City's Central Park. The obelisks in London and Paris are a pair, each measuring 21 metres, while the Paris obelisk is 23 metres tall. Its twin is still in Luxor, Egypt.

The Ancient Egyptians used children as scarecrows

How frightful!

Throughout history, children have done some pretty rotten and very dangerous jobs, from sweeping chimneys to cleaning the fluff from the machines in cotton mills and working as trappers in mines. Their job was to open and close small doors in coalmines to make sure that air flowed freely and they worked for up to 16 HOURS A DAY.

But WHO would use a child as a scarecrow?

★ And the truth is...

The Egyptians, that's who.

It's said that they used slave children as real, live scarecrows, forcing them to stand in fields and scare the birds away from the crops.

SCARY.

Verdict: _____

TRUTH

Ancient Egyptians didn't call their mummies, er, 'mummies'

But what ELSE did they call a dead body that was preserved so it could be used in the afterlife?
(Because imagine the horror if an Egyptian pharaoh travelled to the next world, only to find that he'd gone rotten on the way.)

★ And the truth is...

Disappointingly, the Ancient Egyptians don't seem to have had a special word for an embalmed corpse.

The word 'mummy' comes from the Arabic word 'mummiya', which was invented much later as a word for the black, squishy wax or bitumen used to seal coffins.

Verdict: _____ TRUTH _____

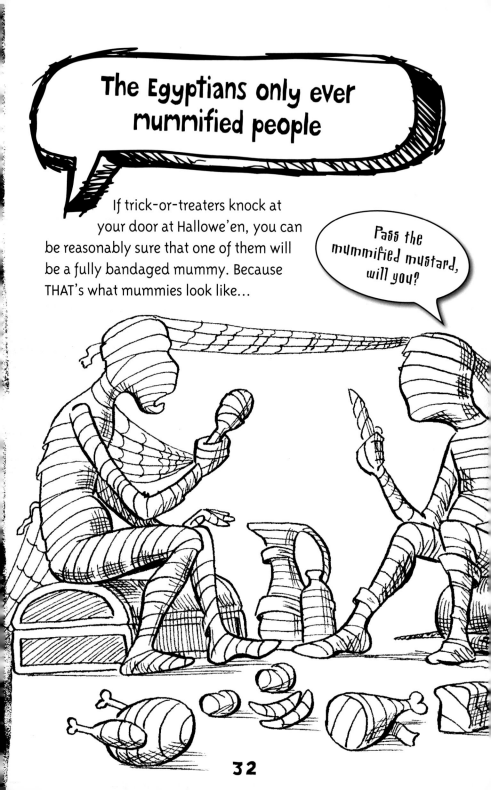

The Egyptians only ever mummified people

If trick-or-treaters knock at your door at Hallowe'en, you can be reasonably sure that one of them will be a fully bandaged mummy. Because THAT's what mummies look like...

Pass the mummified mustard, will you?

★ And the truth is...

... except they don't always.

You might think that the only ones to be mummified in Ancient Egypt were the pharaohs (who were then buried with all their treasure inside huge pyramids or tombs) and other, less-royal people. Not a bit of it. Long ago, the Egyptians mummified pretty much any creature they could get their hands on, including fish, birds, bulls, snakes, monkeys, gazelles, cats, dogs and even crocodiles. And when a pharaoh died, he was buried with his mummified pets too, so they could travel to the afterlife with him.

Mummified animals were a popular gift for the gods and enterprising Egyptians set up businesses that specialised in supplying the many, many animals that were mummified. The demand was SO huge that some species, such as varieties of ibis and baboon, became extinct.

Mummification wasn't limited to living things, either. Mummified fruit, vegetables and joints of meat have also been discovered in tombs, so the dead wouldn't, um, starve in the afterlife.

Amazing eh?

Verdict: —— **BUSTED** ——

PHARAOH PHACT PHILE

FULL NAME: Tutankhamun (he was first called Tutankhaten, but is now known as King Tut)

NATIONALITY: Egyptian

LIVED: circa 1341–1323 BCE

REIGNED: circa 1332–1323 BCE

WIFE: Ankhesenamun, who was also his half-sister. (Marrying their siblings was something that the pharaohs did a lot. Eww.)

WHO WAS TUTANKHAMUN?

He might be the world's best-known mummy, but Tutankhamun only ruled Egypt for ten years, dying at the age of just 18 or 19. He wasn't a big name in Ancient Egyptian history and only really became famous when his tomb was discovered in 1922 in the Valley of the Kings. Unlike many other tombs, which had been ransacked by grave robbers, Tutankhamun's tomb was nearly untouched, meaning that Egyptologists could find out ALL about the young pharaoh, which is why he is so famous.

MOST FAMOUS FOR?

Tutankhamun's gold–and–blue striped death mask has become one of the most recognisable symbols of Ancient Egypt. There are photos and pictures of it EVERYWHERE. But if you want to see it in true life, you'll have to visit the Egypt Museum in Cairo. Sorry.

Someone behind me? Where?

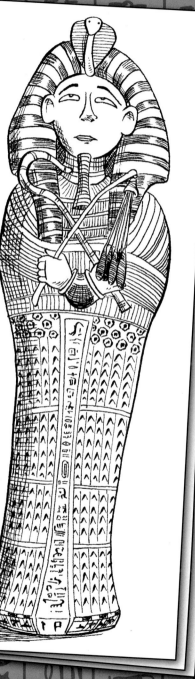

> ## Mummies were once used as medicine

Ha ha!

HILARIOUS.

> Arghhh! Help me mummy!

⭐ And the truth is...

It's no joke. Dead bodies were once used in medicine — and not as long ago as you might think.

Mummies were the medicine of choice for a huge range of illnesses from the 12th century. And it wasn't until the end of the 18th century that the practice, um, died out.

First, the mummy was ground up to a powder, which was then added to liquid to make a medicine. This was supposed to be an excellent treatment for internal bleeding. And bruises. And headaches. And stomach ulcers. When apothecaries — old-fashioned pharmacists — ran out of mummies to grind up, they made new ones. And if there weren't any spare bodies for them to mummify, they simply dug them up.

Verdict:  TRUTH

Pssst! Even KINGS used mummy medicine.

Because the mummies had been preserved for such a long time, it was thought that they might preserve life in living people too. Charles II of England had his own personal collection of mummies and if any tiny bits crumbled off them, he would RUB THEM INTO HIS SKIN. (Ewww.)

The king also sipped a special medicine that was known as The King's Drops, which was made from powdered human skull dissolved in alcohol. (Bleurgh.)

Charles II thought that these fabulously gruesome potions would preserve him from illness and death.

But they didn't.

He still died in 1685.

The Ancient Egyptian civilisation lasted for 2,000 years

Wow. They were around for a loooooong time.

I'm SURE there's a tomb around here somewhere...

★ And the truth is...

Actually, Ancient Egypt lasted for more like 3,000 years. It spanned so many centuries that historians divide it up into chunks of time to make it easier to study. The top three eras were...

The Old Kingdom *2690 BCE–2180 BCE (approx)*
This was also known as the Pyramid Age, because the pharaohs who died back then were each popped in a pyramid. But it took a lot of time and effort to build a pyramid. And after the fabulous structure had been sealed with the pharaoh – and all the treasures they'd need in the afterlife – in it, that pyramid had to be guarded too, which cost money. Because there were a lot of grave robbers about and you couldn't exactly hide a pyramid.

The Middle Kingdom *(2050 BCE–1650 BCE)*
This was Egypt's golden age. By now, the Ancient Egyptians had decided to bury their pharaohs in hidden tombs, which were quicker and cheaper to build and MUCH easier to hide from grave robbers.

The New Kingdom *(1550 BCE–1070 BCE)*
During the New Kingdom, Egypt conquered many of its neighbouring countries and pharaohs became all-powerful. They were all buried in tombs in the Valley of the Kings, near the city of Luxor.

Verdict: — **BUSTED** —

The Ancient Egyptians invented bowling

Really?

Not archery or fishing or javelin or boxing or weightlifting or swimming?

⭐ And the truth is...

Actually, the Ancient Egyptians took part in ALL of these sports and a few more besides. (Like the high jump and rowing and gymnastics and hockey and handball and tug-of-war and running.)

But it's possible that they INVENTED bowling.

Archaeologists have unearthed something that looks very like a modern bowling hall at a building in a town south of Cairo. They have also discovered balls of varying sizes and a lane to hurl them down!

It's enough to bowl you over.

Verdict: Quite possibly  TRUTH

The Egyptians practised human sacrifice

Why would such a sophisticated people as the Ancient Egyptians do such a terrible thing? Human sacrifice is usually carried out so that a person's life can be offered to a god or other being as a sort of gift. But in the case of the Ancient Egyptians, it's said that they didn't kill people so that they could make presents of them; they killed servants so they could travel with them to the afterlife.

★ And the truth is...

When some of the earliest Egyptian pharaohs died, their servants were killed too and buried with them. This was so the servants could continue to serve the pharaoh in the afterlife. Mummified servants have been discovered in the tombs of some of the first pharaohs — one was buried with almost 300 of them! (Perhaps he was particularly lazy.) But fortunately for servants Egypt-wide, the practice died out fairly quickly. And even though the Egyptians were fond of hunting almost every other animal under the sun (see page 60-61), there is little or no evidence of them practising human sacrifice in the later years of the civilisation.

Verdict: A little bit of TRUTH but mostly BUSTED

Sand caused deadly diseases

Sand is lovely to lie on, sink your toes into or build sandcastles from, but it's not the sort of thing you want to get in your eyes. Or your sandwiches. Or your, um, sandals.

But sand is not actually harmful, is it?

⭐ And the truth is...

Egypt is mostly desert — the Western Desert alone covers two-thirds of the country — which means there's an awful lot of sand.

Very old medical texts show that the Ancient Egyptians were plagued by coughs. (They treated these with a delicious-sounding mixture of herbs and honey. Yum.) So were the coughs caused by breathing in sand?

No. Scientists have discovered evidence of tuberculosis (a nasty lung disease) in an Egyptian mummy, so it was probably this, rather than sand, that made the Egyptians cough.

Verdict: **BUSTED**

Tax avoidance was punishable by death

Wow.

Not a fine or a jail term?
Isn't death a bit HARSH?

★ And the truth is...

No, no, no. Of *course* the Ancient Egyptians didn't kill tax dodgers!

They just chopped off an ear instead.

(Or a nose.)

But Ancient Egyptians who didn't pay their taxes weren't the only ones to get it in the neck (or ear or nose). Check out these other shocking punishments...

 If a weaver took a day off work he could be whipped 50 times.

Stealing an animal hide meant 100 blows.

And if an Egyptian man was caught stealing a whole cow, he was impaled upon a sharp stake and left there to die. Oh, and his wife and children were sold into slavery too.

YIKES.

Verdict:

the
CURIOUS TIMES

NAPOLEON AND THE GREAT PYRAMID

Napoleon Bonaparte was the Emperor of France from 1804 to 1814. He was also pretty big in the army and spent a lot of time conquering foreign lands. And it was while invading Egypt in 1798 that Something Very Mysterious happened to the French leader.

SIGHTSEEING

It's rumoured that while exploring the chambers inside the Great Pyramid – because there's always time

Below: The pyramids a long time ago...

for sightseeing while you're invading another country – Napoleon asked to be left inside the pharaoh's chamber.

ALONE

When he later emerged from the chamber, Napoleon is said to have looked shocked and shaken. But he refused to say what had happened inside the tomb and banned everyone from ever mentioning the incident again.

DEATHBED

Years later, on his deathbed, Napoleon was visited by a friend who asked what had happened inside the pyramid.

For a moment, it looked as if Napoleon was about to reveal all, but then he apparently said, 'What's the use? You'd never believe me.'

And he never told a soul.

SO WHAT?

So what did happen? Did the ghost of the long-dead pharaoh predict Napoleon's future? Did the French leader step through a portal into Ancient Egypt? Did he step in mummified camel poo?

We'll never know.

Above: Napoleon scratching his tummy (again).

It took months to make a mummy

Oh, come on. All the Ancient Egyptians had to do was wind bandages round their dead pharaoh. How long is THAT going to take?

Empty the body, dry the body, stuff the body, wrap the body. Yep, I think that's everything.

★ And the truth is...

Believe it or not, mummification — the process of preserving a body — took the embalmer* at least 70 DAYS, if he was doing it the Ancient Egyptian way. The Egyptians thought that if a person wasn't mummified after death, he or she would never reach the afterlife, so it was important to make a really good job of it. This is why mummies in museums are often in such good condition, even now.

The embalmer was the person who carried out the careful process of mummification, making sure that the dead body did not rot away.

Verdict: _____ **TRUTH** _____

HOW TO MAKE A MUMMY

**(But REALLY don't try this at home. Or in Egypt.
Or anywhere, really.)**

1 Lay the dead body inside a tent, because dead bodies get REALLY STINKY in the heat and Egypt is a hot place.

2 Remove the dead body's brain, by simply sticking a long hook up the person's nose and YANKING IT OUT. Yes, really.

3 Take out any internal organs that might go off quickly, making sure to leave the heart inside.

4 Separate the stomach, the liver, the lungs and the intestines and plop them into canopic jars – special containers that would be buried with the finished mummy later.

5 Dry out the body by covering it with salt, to soak up all the moisture.

6 Stuff the body with linen to make it look a bit more, um, lifelike.

7 Now add some false eyes. Stones will do. Onions are even better (see page 89).

8 Now wrap with HUNDREDS OF METRES of linen, taking care to wrap each finger and toe individually.

9 If you like, put a mask of the person's face on top of their face bandages and put the body in a coffin that you made earlier.

10 Seventy days later, your mummy is complete. Now all you have to do is collect the hundreds of things that they might need to survive in the afterlife and put the mummy and everything else inside the pyramid.

You did remember to build the pyramid, didn't you...?

Mummies were buried with their mouths open

If eating with your mouth open is rude and staring at things with your mouth open makes you look GORMLESS, then why would the Ancient Egyptians want to be mummified with their mouths open and look like that FOR EVER?

★ And the truth is...

Mummies were buried or entombed with their mouths wide open to make sure they'd still be able to eat, drink and talk in the next life, of course.

Once a corpse had been mummified, a priest would perform an opening-of-the-mouth ceremony. This involved touching the mummy's mouth with an axe and then a chisel, rubbing its face with milk and hugging it. Afterwards, Ancient Egyptians believed the mummy would be able to eat, drink and move around as normal in the afterlife.

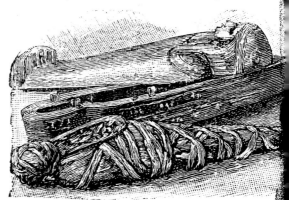

Verdict:

PHARAOH PHACT PHILE

FULL NAME: Hatshepsut

NATIONALITY: Egyptian

LIVED: circa 1508–1458 BCE

REIGNED: 1479–1458 BCE

HUSBAND: Thutmose II (who, in true Ancient-Egyptian style, was also her half-brother).

WHO WAS HATSHEPSUT?

Hatshepsut was the greatest female Egyptian pharaoh OF ALL TIME.* The daughter of Thutmose I, Hatshepsut married her half-brother Thutmose II and they reigned together until his death. Hatshepsut's nephew (and stepson) Thutmose III was next in line for the throne, but he was just a boy and far too young to be in charge. So Hatshepsut rushed to the rescue and offered to rule in her nephew's place until Thutmose III was old enough to be pharaoh. Except she sort of never gave the throne back.

Hatshepsut's reign was a successful one. She built grand temples and obelisks, the Egyptian economy boomed and she brought back gold, ivory and myrrh from a trip abroad.

No one is exactly sure what happened to Hatshepsut, but once he was properly in power, Thutmose III tried to destroy all references to his aunt (who was also his stepmother, of course). Whether he was cross with her or just trying to show that HE was in charge now, nobody knows.

* Cleopatra (see page 78-79) was also pretty fabulous, but as she was Greek, she could hardly be a great Egyptian.

Of course I'll give you your throne back!

Ancient Egyptians snacked on hedgehogs

Just imagine crunching on all those spikes! It would be like, um… eating a hedgehog. Ouch AND yuck. (And, actually, ewwwww too.)

Surely the Ancient Egyptians didn't EAT hedgehogs?

⭐ And the truth is…

They certainly did.

Hedgehog WAS an ingredient in some Ancient Egyptian recipes. (So perhaps it wasn't as prickly as you'd expect.) But more often, rich Egyptians feasted on beef, goat, mutton, perch, catfish, mullet, goose, duck and heron.

Meanwhile, poor Egyptians ate mainly bread. (But not hedgehog sandwiches.)

Awww.

Verdict: **TRUTH**

Ancient Egyptian illnesses were caused by evil spirits

Not germs?

Or bugs passed on by other people?

Or just plain, old-fashioned bad luck?

It was actually EVIL SPIRITS that made the Ancient Egyptians ill?

★ And the truth is...

This is clearly nonsense. Ancient Egyptians became ill because of poor hygiene, bacteria, viruses and poor diet, so pretty much the same things that make people ill now.

But, because the Ancient Egyptians knew much less about the human body than we do today, they assumed that evil spirits were to blame for any health problems. They wore amulets to protect themselves against disease and injury, and turned to magical remedies and spells when they did fall ill. To be fair, some of these remedies probably did less harm than actual Ancient Egyptian medicine.

Verdict: ——— BUSTED ———

HOW THE ANCIENT EGYPTIANS CURED

THE COMMON COLD!

You will need:
Breast milk from a woman who has given birth to a boy.

Er, that's it.

How to treat the patient:
But here's the REALLY MAGICAL bit. While the patient is gulping away, recite this ancient spell to chase the cold away...

May you flow out, catarrh, son of catarrh, who breaks the bones, who destroys the skull, who hacks in the marrow, who causes the seven openings in the head to ache.

That'll do the trick.

Or so says the Ebers Papyrus, an Ancient Egyptian scroll that includes 700 medicines and treatments and spells to rid people of all sorts of illnesses. Experts think that the ideas it contains may be an astonishing 5,500 years old.

But as well as the frankly bizarre treatments they used — such as how to cure death with half an onion and the froth from a pint of beer — the Ancient Egyptians did know about the human body. They knew about the heart, the pulse, the spleen, the lungs, the brain, the nose and about bone structure too. And they stitched wounds with a needle and thread.

True, the Ancient Egyptians didn't ALWAYS get it right, but they were starting to understand how the human body works and how to fix it if it went wrong. Anything they didn't understand, they fixed with, um, magic.

The Ancient Egyptians could fix broken bones

Hmm. If the Ancient Egyptians treated asthma with garlic and onions, and used boiled porcupine spines to promote hair growth (for another even more bizarre cure for baldness, see page 24), they were hardly going to be any good at mending broken bones...

Or were they?

★ **And the truth is...**

Yes, they were.

Ancient Egyptian doctors could set broken bones with no problem at all. We know this because archaeologists have found actual proof — skeletons with broken bones that had been properly set and were as good as new.

Verdict: _____ **TRUTH** _____

Ancient Egyptian eye make-up was better than medicine

The Ancient Egyptians invented make-up that made the wearer look good AND made them super-healthy at the same time?

Wow. That's some make-up!

But can it possibly be true?

★ And the truth is...

Black eye make-up — also known as kohl — was made from lead sulphide, which was both a disinfectant and an insect repellent. It was also said to protect the Ancient Egyptians' eyes from the sun.

But green eye make-up went one better. It was made from malachite powder, which helped to protect eyes from infection.

Perhaps the Egyptians weren't just pretty faces after all...?

Verdict:  TRUTH

Paddling in a river was bad for your health

Oh, come on. REALLY?

What could possibly be wrong with a lovely paddle in one of the longest rivers in the world and, in fact, the ONLY river to flow through Egypt all year round? (This is the River Nile, of course. It's 6,853 km long, flows through Burundi, Democratic Republic of the Congo, Ethiopia, Kenya, Rwanda, South Sudan, Sudan, Tanzania and Uganda. Oh, and Egypt.)

⭐ And the truth is...

In Ancient Egyptian times, the River Nile was teeming with parasites. (A parasite is a living thing that lives on or inside another living thing, which is known as the host. The parasite feeds from the host to survive. **Ewww**.) Schistosoma was one type of parasite that was very common in Ancient Egyptian waterways. It was a tiny wormlike creature that burrowed into the skin of unsuspecting paddlers, laying eggs inside them. (Yuck.)

It gets worse. Once inside their lovely, comfortable, nutritious host – that's the paddling Ancient Egyptian – parasites like the female guinea worm could grow as long as ONE METRE. And as they grew and grew, they caused damage as they travelled through the host's organs, making them weaker and weaker, and more likely to catch nasty diseases. When the guinea worm was fully grown, it would leave the body by burrowing its way back out through the skin. (Yikes.)

Lunch!

Verdict:

59

Hippos were used as crocodile bait in the Nile

Hippos are dangerous beasts.

Crocodiles are dangerous beasts.

Using one to lure the other to their death would surely be the most dangerous — and the MEANEST — sport of all time?

⭐ And the truth is...

Fortunately, the Ancient Egyptians were not lunatics. They didn't use one wild animal to catch another. But they WERE keen hunters, and they did try to catch both hippos and crocodiles on the Nile.

Just not at the same time.

When they went crocodile hunting, Ancient Egyptians used a pig on a hook as bait (which makes using worms to catch fish seem positively dull by comparison). They made a piglet squeal on the riverbank to catch the crocodile's attention. Then, when the crocodile swam over to investigate... and SNAPPED, they reeled it in. (Presumably in an enormous, crocodile-proof net.)

Hippos were a totally different matter.

Hippo hunters didn't mess around with nets and pigs. Instead they simply lassoed the beasts in the water. It was a dangerous sport though — if the Ancient Egyptians fell in, there was a high chance they'd be a VERY angry hippo's lunch.

Crocodiles and hippos were not the only animals the Egyptians liked to hunt. They went after everything, from lions and leopards to elephants and ostriches.

NEVER take an Ancient Egyptian to the zoo.

Verdict: ── **BUSTED** ──

Ancient Egyptian gods and goddesses wore fancy-dress masks

The Ancient Egyptians didn't just worship one being. They worshipped HUNDREDS of them. Each god or goddess stood for something different — such as the sun or wind or wisdom — which meant that it was much easier to send prayers in exactly the right direction.

Of course, with so many gods and goddesses, how did the Ancient Egyptians tell them apart? Did the deities really wear fancy-dress masks, so it was easier to recognise them?

⭐ And the truth is...

Oh no.

These weren't masks. They were actual animal HEADS.

Many Ancient Egyptian gods and goddesses were half-person, half-animal. For example, Amun, who was the king of all the gods, had the head of a ram. Horus, the god of the sky, had the head of a falcon. And Sekmet, goddess of war and battle, had the head of a lioness.

Images of the gods and goddesses adorned the walls of pharaohs' tombs, maybe so they could have a sneak preview of the deities they would meet in the afterlife.

Verdict: — **BUSTED** —

Pyramids can be seen from space

The Great Pyramid of Giza — also known as the Pyramid of Khufu — is about 139 metres tall, which is equal to the height of one-and-a-half Statues of Liberty.

But space is very far away. Is the Great Pyramid REALLY great big?

★ And the truth is...

The International Space Station (ISS) orbits Earth at a distance of about 400 km above the surface of the planet. But even though that's VERY far, it is totally true that astronauts on board are able to see all three of the Great Pyramids of Giza from the ISS. They've even taken photographs of them and popped them online. (Have a look. They're GREAT shots.)

But why are three pyramids built so close to each other? Egypt is pretty big. It's not like they didn't have plenty of room.

The fact is that after Khufu had built the Great Pyramid of Giza for himself, his son Khafre decided that he'd like one too. So he built one next door, maybe so they could keep each other company in the afterlife. When Khafre's son Menkaure was in power, he built a third.

(None of the three pharaohs built their own pyramids, of course. They had workers to do that. Quite a lot of workers. Experts disagree on exactly how many people it took to construct each pyramid, but it may have been at least 14,000 and possibly as many as 200,000. Wow.)

Verdict:  TRUTH

Pssst! The Pyramid of Khufu is the largest of the three Great Pyramids of Giza and the only one of the Seven Wonders of the Ancient World that's still in reasonably good shape today. But just as humans shrink a little as they grow older, so has the pyramid...

When it was built over 4,500 years ago, the Great Pyramid of Giza measured over 146 metres tall. But the smooth stone surface that once covered it has been worn away to reveal the blocks beneath, which is why it is now so much shorter. It's still quite big though, which is why astronauts can see it from space.

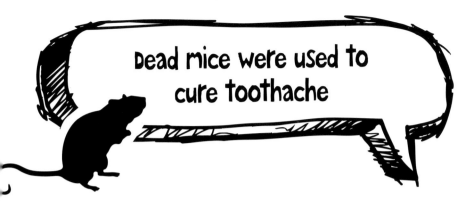

Dead mice were used to cure toothache

Ancient Egyptians didn't have painkillers.

But they had to use SOMETHING to sort out toothache.

 And the truth is...

Unfortunately for Ancient Egyptians with toothache, a common remedy was half a dead mouse — its body still warm — pressed against the aching tooth.

Other equally useless remedies involved earthworms boiled in oil, bread dough, incense and fennel seeds.

Aren't you glad you live in the 21st century?

Verdict: ___ TRUTH ___

PHARAOH PHACT PHILE

FULL NAME: Thutmose III

NATIONALITY: Egyptian

LIVED: No-one knows!

REIGNED: 1479–1425 BCE (including 22 years when his aunt Hatshepsut was actually in charge – to find out more, see p50–51)

WIVES: Satiah, Merytre-Hatshepsut, Nebtu, Menwi, Merti and Menhet. He may have married Neferure (his half-sister) too. So that makes a grand total of either six or seven wives. All at the same time, naturally.

WHAT'S THE STORY?
Once Thutmose III had managed to wrestle his throne back from his aunt (who was also his stepmother, remember), he immediately began to make up for lost time. Empire building was at the top of his to-do list and during his reign, Thutmose III

carried out 17 campaigns, conquering lands from modern-day Syria in the north to modern-day Sudan in the south.

The reason historians know so much about Thutmose's military victories is because his scribe and army commander Thanuny made a note of EVERYTHING. All of Thutmose's campaigns are recorded in detail on the inner wall of the great chamber of the Temple of Amun at Karnak, in Egypt.

MOST FAMOUS FOR?

Being ousted by his aunt, Hatshepsut. Oh, and winning wars.

'Pharaoh' means 'king'

The word 'pharaoh' isn't just an exceedingly tricky word to spell. Long, long ago, an Egyptian pharaoh was a royal ruler, just like a king. Pharaohs were head of not just a royal family, but of a country, too. So it stands to reason that their official titles mean the same thing.

Doesn't it...?

★ And the truth is...

Poppycock.

The word 'pharaoh' originally meant 'great house', and referred to the ruler's palace. But because it wasn't the done thing for Egyptians to call their king by his name, they developed a series of nicknames they could use to refer to him. And the word 'pharaoh' was never used to address an Egyptian king directly — instead, it was the word his subjects would use when talking about him.

Besides, pharaohs were both men AND women, so 'pharaoh' couldn't have meant just 'king'. So there.

Verdict: BUSTED

Pyramid workers were the first people EVER to go on strike

Today, striking is a way for employees to protest when they think their wages and working conditions are unfair. But did the Ancient Egyptians get there first?

★ And the truth is...

Ancient Egyptian workers didn't just go on strike — they invented it. Even though they regarded the pharaoh as a living god, this did not stop them protesting for better working conditions. And in the 12th century BCE, during the reign of Ramesses III, when labourers building the royal tomb did not receive their usual payment of grain, they organised the first recorded strike in history. The protest took the form of a sit-in — they refused to leave until their complaints were heard. It worked, and the labourers received their overdue rations.

Hurray!

Verdict: **TRUTH**

Better pay for tomb digging!

Pyramids have supernatural powers

It's said that pyramids are just a little bit magical, and that they can preserve food, keep razor blades sharp and help you stay fit and healthy.

So does PYRAMID POWER actually exist?

⭐ And the truth is...

When French shopkeeper Antoine Bovis visited the Great Pyramid of Giza in the 1930s, he discovered something Seriously Strange inside.

A dead cat.

OK, this may not sound strange, but the odd thing about this dead cat was that its body had not rotted away. It was as if the pyramid itself had preserved, or mummified, it.

Baffled Bovis went away and carried out an experiment with a smaller pyramid, but an equally dead cat. The same thing happened.

Years later, researchers in the USA and Europe tried the experiment again, with exactly the same results. They also discovered that as well as keeping dead cats fresh, the pyramid preserved food, kept razor blades super sharp and helped wounds to heal faster.

They named this pyramid power PYRAMIDOLOGY.

However, despite all of these experiments, no one was able to prove if the pyramid was responsible for all of these magical effects. And if it was responsible, how pyramid power actually worked.

Verdict: _____ you decide!

The Ancient Egyptians preferred wigs to real hair

Oh, come on.

Keep your hair on.

⭐ And the truth is...

Absolutely. The Ancient Egyptians didn't seem to like their own hair at all. There are two reasons for this...

1. Egypt is a **Very Hot Place**. And a fancy hairdo is only going to make a hot head hotter. It was much easier to shave it all off to reveal a lovely cool scalp and then pop on a wig for special occasions.

2. Nits. The Ancient Egyptians were hot on hygiene. And they went to great lengths — or, actually, quite short lengths — to make their heads super-inhospitable places for head lice. If there was no hair on their heads, there was nowhere for nits to live.

   But they still wanted to look good, which is why the Ancient Egyptians wore fabulous wigs instead.

Verdict: TRUTH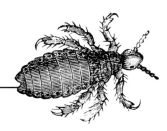

Pharaohs never let their hair down

Well, have YOU ever seen a pharaoh's hair?

If you check out the images of pharaohs that have made it to the 21st century, you won't see any fancy hairdos... but you will see a lot of elaborate, striped headdresses instead.

So what about their hair? Did pharaohs never let it down?

 And the truth is...

A pharaoh's headdress was called a 'nemes' and, like a fake beard, it showed the Ancient Egyptians who was in charge. The cobra that reared at the front of a nemes was supposed to protect the pharaoh from enemies, by spitting fire at them.

As for pharaohs letting their hair or their wigs down, perhaps they did. But if so, they made sure that it wasn't included on any official statues.

Verdict:  TRUTH

The Ancient Egyptians wore 'fat hats'

WHAT?

A hat made of fat?

Surely greasy, sticky, gooey fat was the last thing Ancient Egyptians wanted to pop on top of their hair? In June, July and August, the temperature in Luxor can soar above 40°C. And fat has a habit of melting in the heat...

★ **And the truth is...**

At parties, Ancient Egyptians did wear fat hats on top of their fancy wigs. The cone-shaped hats were made of tallow — a type of animal fat — and myrrh, which was a sweet-smelling resin that came from the commiphora myrrha tree. In the heat, the scented hats slowly melted, so that the Ancient Egyptian's wig remained sweet-smelling for the entire party.

Verdict: ——— TRUTH ———

Ancient Egyptians put toilets in their tombs

Dead people don't wee. Fact.

So why on earth would the Ancient Egyptians have thought they needed to install a toilet in a tomb?

★ And the truth is...

Ancient Egyptian burial rites and customs made sure that the dead person had everything — that's EVERYTHING — they could possibly need in the next life and in some cases this did include a toilet. What's more, the toilet was actually plumbed in, ready for use.

There was a sink too, of course. Because if dead Ancient Egyptians were going to go to the toilet, they would absolutely need to wash their hands afterwards.

Verdict:  TRUTH

PHARAOH PHACT PHILE

FULL NAME: Cleopatra VII Thea Philopater

NATIONALITY: Greek

LIVED: circa 69–30 BCE

REIGNED: 51–30 BCE

HUSBANDS AND BOYFRIEND:
Ptolemy XIII (who was also her brother),
Ptolemy XIV (another brother),
Julius Caesar (not her brother but a Roman emperor – hurray!) and Mark Antony (a Roman general).

CHILDREN:
Caesarion (his father was Julius Caesar – the clue's in the name there), Alexander and Cleopatra (twins), and Ptolemy.

WHO WAS CLEOPATRA?
She was Ancient Egypt's most famous female pharaoh – a member of the Ptolemaic Dynasty, which was a

family of Greek origin that ruled Egypt from 305 to 30 BCE. She was also Ancient Egypt's last proper pharaoh.

Cleopatra was famous enough to inspire William Shakespeare's play, **Antony and Cleopatra**. (It's a tragedy. Take tissues.) And she was pretty big in Hollywood too – **Cleopatra**, starring Elizabeth Taylor, was the box-office smash of 1963, but it cost so much to make that it never made any money.

MOST FAMOUS FOR?

Finishing herself off with an asp's bite. Or did she? See page 27 to find out THE TRUTH.

What is an asp anyway?

79

Napoleon's troops blasted off the Sphinx's nose

The Great Sphinx of Giza is an enormous statue of a mythical creature — with the body of a lion and a human head — that sits close to the Pyramids of Giza (see page 64-66) and near the banks of the River Nile. It's quite famous. You've probably seen photos of it (and if not, check them out).

But the really bizarre thing about this hybrid creature is that it has NO NOSE.

And the rumour on the streets is that the Sphinx's hooter was destroyed by Napoleon's troops, when they fired a cannonball at it. Whoops.

★ And the truth is...

The Sphinx's original limestone nose was one metre wide, so it would've needed something Very Big to get rid of it, but Napoleon's troops weren't to blame for the simple reason that the nose was already missing before they arrived in Egypt in 1798.

The truth is more likely to be that the Sphinx's nose vanished in the 14th century because of a chap called Muhammad Sa'im al-Dahr. He was reportedly outraged that the locals made offerings to the Sphinx — in an effort to prevent flooding that would ruin their crops — and he prised off the nose.

Probably.

Verdict: **BUSTED**

It was against the law to kill a cat

Excellent. Top marks go to the Ancient Egyptians for their animal protection skills!

⭐ And the truth is...

The Ancient Egyptians loved cats. REALLY loved cats. In fact, they loved cats so much that anyone who harmed a cat was in serious trouble with the law.

The Egyptians' love of cats probably began when they noticed how wild cats protected their crops from vermin. They began to domesticate the animals, welcoming them into their homes and feeding them. There, cats helped out by getting rid of mice and rats. And SNAKES. Yikes.

Soon, cats had achieved god-like status.

The Ancient Egyptians made bronze statues of them.

They painted pictures of them.

They even MUMMIFIED them.

So it's not surprising that the punishment for killing a cat was... DEATH.

Verdict:  _____

> **Pssst!** If you ever visit Paris, don't miss the collection of cat mummies at the Musée du Louvre.

During a battle, soldiers chopped bits off dead enemy soldiers

This sounds both gruesome and weird. What use could the Ancient Egyptians possibly have had for a load of dead enemy arms and legs?

That's 2 arms, 1 head and 1 leg. Excellent work!

⭐ And the truth is...

It was all because of statistics.

The Ancient Egyptians liked to keep records of things. Lots of things. They even employed scribes to make sure that everything was properly written down. Wills, family trees, the size of crops, accounts, magic spells and formal letters were just a few of the many things that it was a scribe's job to write about. But perhaps one of the scribe's most bloodthirsty tasks took place on the battlefield...

Ancient Egyptians also wanted to keep track of how many enemy soldiers they had fought, defeated and killed. But in the heat of the battle, a head count of the dead was tricky — anyone adding up the dead was in serious danger of being killed themselves. So the Ancient Egyptians came up with a novel solution. When they killed an enemy, soldiers would cut off an arm, leg or other — ahem — part of their body. Then, once the fighting was safely over, scribes would trek the battlefield and count up the severed body parts. Then the Egyptians knew how many soldiers they had vanquished.

Dead easy, huh?

Verdict: _____ **TRUTH** _____

Ancient Egyptian soldiers were as young as ten

A ten-year-old soldier.

Surely that is both BAD and WRONG?

★ And the truth is...

Amazingly, by the time a child reached ten, they might already have been in the army for FIVE YEARS.

Once a family had decided that a child was to have a military career, the child was signed up. Children joined up when they were as young as five, though their actual time in the army didn't begin until much later, when they were 20 years old.

Life in the army was good. Ancient Egyptian soldiers were well treated and if they were lucky enough to survive the battles in which they fought, and live long enough, soldiers were even entitled to an army pension.

Verdict:  **BUSTED**

The Ancient Egyptian police employed monkeys

Police dogs? Yes.

Police horses? Yes.

> Will you STOP monkeying around!

Police MONKEYS? Ha ha ha ha ha ha ha!

How totally ridiculous.

★ And the truth is...

One of the Ancient Egyptian police's most important jobs was supervising marketplaces, which were hotbeds of crime. Markets were packed with thieves, looking for something to steal.

Police monkeys were trained to chase criminals and then to catch them (with a little help from humans).

Verdict: **TRUTH**

Pssst! This wasn't the only job carried out by monkeys. The Ancient Egyptians also trained Ethiopian baboons to climb trees and pick dates!

HOW THE ANCIENT EGYPTIANS ~~CURED~~ FIXED

A BROKEN MUMMY!

Mummification was a tricky process and things could – and did – go wrong. But don't panic. Quick-thinking embalmers could fix ANYTHING.

Mummy mistake: head bandaged too tightly.

Result: nose broken or squashed.

Solution: two rolls of papyrus (paper made from reeds) pushed up the nostrils to keep the nose's shape.

Mummy mistake: body handled too roughly.

Result: head snapped off.

Solution: spear the head back on using a big pointy stick.

Mummy mistake: too much padding shoved inside the body.

Result: body bursts open like an overstuffed teddy bear.

Solution: simply stitch it up and tighten the bandages.

 Mummy mistake: eyes damaged.

Result: eyes have to be popped out.

Solution: pop in false eyes made from onions.

SORTED!

Ancient Egyptian hieroglyphs were decoded using a stone

A stone? That's all?

Don't code-breakers usually use something a bit fancier to crack codes? Like the Colossus computers at Bletchley Park during World War Two or cipher machines or really whizzy maths?

Try your hand at this code, kids!

ROSETTA STONE

⭐ And the truth is...

Before the 19th century, no one could read Ancient Egyptian hieroglyphs — picture writing in which the pictures stand for words or syllables or sounds — so the Rosetta Stone was one of the most important discoveries EVER. It was the key that cracked the code of the Ancient Egyptian hieroglyphic language. And it worked in a startlingly simple way.

Made of granite-like rock, the Rosetta Stone was inscribed with three chunks of text. The top text was in Ancient Egyptian hieroglyphs, the middle text was Demotic and the bottom text was in Ancient Greek.

And because all three texts said EXACTLY THE SAME THING, but in different languages, and because scholars and historians in the 19th century could still understand Ancient Greek, it was possible to match the Ancient Egyptian hieroglyphs with the Ancient Greek and, from there, slowly work out the entire hieroglyphic alphabet.

Now, Ancient Egyptian writing was no longer a mystery. And it was all because of a lump of stone.

Verdict:  TRUTH

 **Alors!** The Rosetta Stone was discovered in 1799 by one of Napoleon's troops during the French leader's expedition to Egypt. They later gave it up to British troops and it's now on display in the British Museum in London.

the CURIOUS TIMES

PERPLEXING PYRAMIDS

Pyramids are enormous structures, made from exceedingly heavy stone blocks. Yet they were also constructed thousands of years before cranes were invented by the Ancient Greeks.

So how exactly did the Ancient Egyptians do it?

Did they use a straight – or perhaps spiral – ramp coated with mud and water so that the stone blocks could be pushed up the pyramid easily and then slotted into place?

This is a great theory, but any ramp would have had to be nearly two kilometres long to reach the top at a reasonable gradient (if it was too steep, it would have been impossible to push the blocks upwards).

Or did they use levers, wooden sledges and papyrus ropes to drag the blocks to their final destinations?

Again, it's a fabulous idea, but it would have been VERY hard work. The truth is that no one knows exactly how the pyramids were built. Although we do know one thing – the Ancient Egyptians made a really good job of it. There aren't many structures that are still standing over 4,500 years after they were built.

Cleopatra bathed in milk

It's said that Ancient Egypt's most glamorous pharaoh bathed in the milk of 700 asses (a relation of the donkey) EVERY DAY!

★ And the truth is...

Although no one is sure that Cleo actually bathed in milk, it does seem that the legend may be true. Lactic acid (found in milk) is a type of alpha-hydroxy acid (AHA), which is used by the beauty industry today. It's supposed to be good for reducing wrinkles and generally making skin look great.

So perhaps clever Cleopatra had already worked this out, 2,000 years ago!

Verdict: Probably  TRUTH

Where can I find myths about...

100%
SUCKER-PROOF

GUARANTEED!

Take a look at our other marvellously mythbusting titles...

Tip:
Turn over!